Letterland

My name is

Let's learn about...

u_e ue oo ew   ar or

er ir ur wr   o oo u

oy oi aw au ow ou

Level 2 - Workbook 2

Can you hear Mr U in these words? Circle the object in which you can't hear Mr U saying his name.

Think of a '**u_e**' word and draw it.

Draw a line around the '**u_e**' words in the grid below. They go across and down.

o	d	s	c	e	g	v
w	a	t	u	n	e	f
k	d	i	b	a	m	l
t	u	b	e	g	y	u
z	n	x	r	o	p	t
p	e	r	f	u	m	e

dune

flute

cube

tube

perfume

Can you find one more '**u_e**' word in the grid? Copy it on to the lines.

___ ___ ___ ___ ___

Write '**u_e**' on the lines to complete these words.

 fl__t

 perf__m__

 parach__t

 t__b

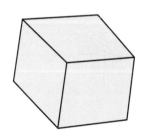 c__b

Find the objects that include Mr U and Mr E out walking. Tick a box as you find each one.

Tuesday

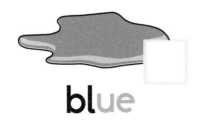

blue

glue

Draw lines from Mr U and Mr E to the things that include them out walking. Circle the one that doesn't.

BLUEBELL AVENUE

Fondue Party!
Venue:
Bluebell Avenue
Tuesday

Think of an '**ue**' word and draw it.

Red Robot needs rescuing! Look at the pictures below and draw a circle around each difference in picture 2.

Find the objects that include the Boot and Foot Twins. Tick a box as you find each one.

z⊙⊙   ball⊙⊙n   b⊙⊙t

Draw lines from the Boot and Foot Twins to the things that include them. Circle the one that doesn't.

Think of an '**oo**' word and draw it.

Write '**oo**' or '**ue**' on the line to complete these words.

oo   ue

bl_____

oo   ue

z_____

oo   ue

b_____ t

oo   ue

gl_____

Draw lines from Eddy and Walter to the things that include them saying their new sound. Circle the one that doesn't.

Think of an '**ew**' word and draw it.

Draw lines to join the jigsaw pieces to their place in the big picture.

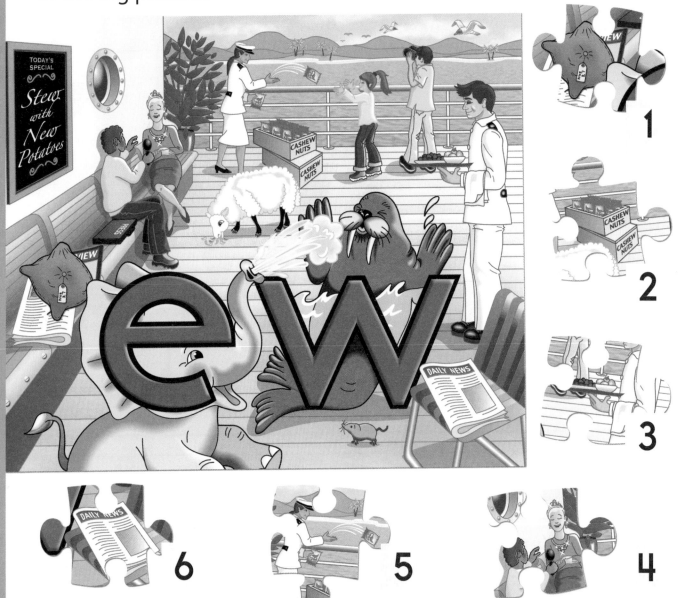

Which '**ew**' word can you see in picture 6? Write it on the lines.

____ ____ ____ ____

Draw lines to join each picture to the correct word.

news

jewels

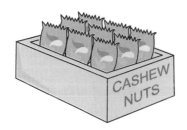

cashews

stew

chew

Use your stickers to label the picture below. Look back in your book if you need help remembering the words.

Write down where this scene is.

At the _____

Listen

Fill in the missing letters to complete the sentences below. Then listen and repeat the sentences.

Track 115

Mmmm... n_ _dles!

She gl_ _s on a n_ _ r_ _f.

Fred can play a t_n_ on his fl_t_.

The twins think he is c_ _l!

15

Listen

 Listen to the words and put a tick next to the one you hear. The first one has been done for you.

 Track 116

1.  ✓    FOOD ☐    ☐

2.  ☐    ☐    ☐

3.  ☐    ☐    ☐

4.  ☐    ☐    ☐

5.  ☐    ☐    ☐

Listen again This exercise requires careful listening skills. Listen more than once if you need to.

Listen

Listen to the words. Put a tick next to the correct spelling pattern. The first one has been done for you.

Track 117

How do you spell it?

1.  ✔️  ☐ ☐

2.  ☐  ☐ ☐

3.  ☐  ☐ ☐

4.  ☐  ☐ ☐

5.  ☐   ☐ ☐

4 spellings: 1 sound This exercise requires very careful listening skills. Listen at least twice before trying to complete it.

Can you hear Arthur Ar in these words? Circle the object in which you can't hear Arthur Ar saying his last name.

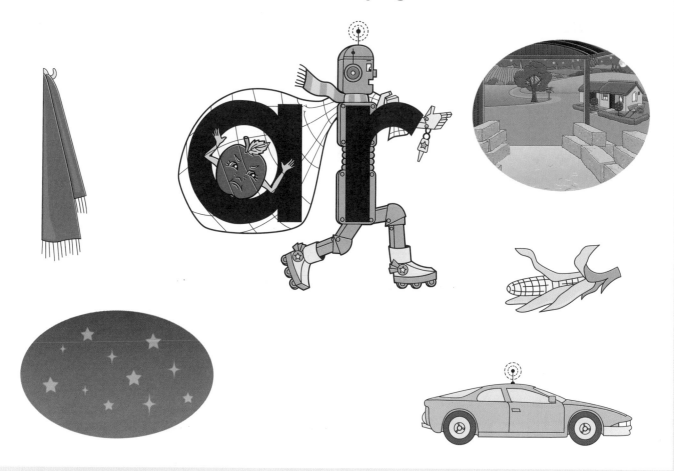

Think of an 'ar' word and draw it.

What's on the card?

Arthur Ar has sent us a postcard. Circle all the '**ar**' words on the card.

9th March

I went to the farm in my car.

To

_____

Write your name on the line.

Where did Arthur Ar go in his car?
Circle the correct answer.

the stars

the garden

the farm

Circle the '**ar**' word that rhymes in each row.

shark

ship

park

sock

star

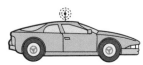

car

sack

stop

farm

four

fan

arm

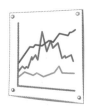

chart

cheese

start

chair

20

Can you hear Orvil Or in these words? Circle the object in which you can't hear Orvil Or saying his last name.

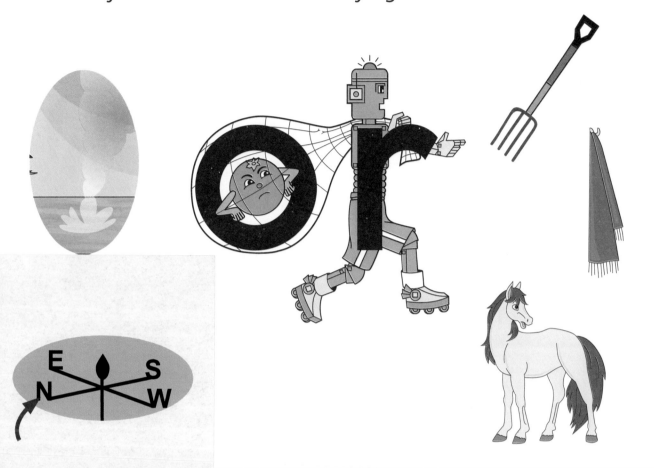

Think of an '**or**' word and draw it.

Draw a line around the '**or**' words in the grid below. They go across and down.

s	h	o	r	t	s	e
t	o	n	o	r	t	h
i	r	a	u	f	a	l
k	s	m	c	o	r	n
r	e	f	o	r	t	y
o	r	w	o	k	v	z

horse

corn

shorts

forty

fork

Can you find one more '**or**' word in the grid? Copy it on to the lines.

___ ___ ___ ___ ___

Look at the pictures below and draw a circle around each difference in picture 2.

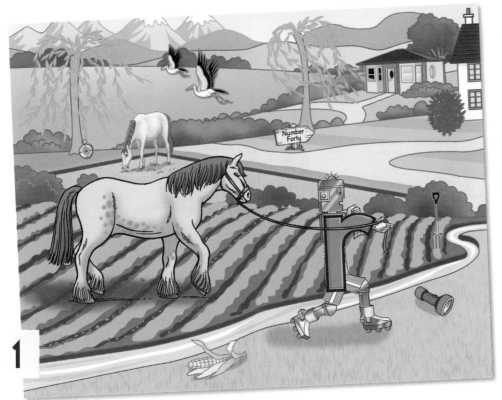

Find the objects that include Ernest Er,
the elephant stealer. Tick a box as you find each one.

WILDLIFE PARK

DANGER

Herbs

tiger ☐

ladder ☐

painter ☐

Can you hear Ernest Er in these words? Circle the object in which you can't hear Ernest Er saying his last name.

Think of an '**er**' word and draw it.

Write '**er**' on the lines to complete these words.

 ladd_____

 tig_____

 f_____n

 dang_____

 flow_____

Find the objects that include Irving Ir, the ink stealer.
Tick a box as you find each one.

bird ☐

shirt ☐

skirt ☐

Can you hear Irving Ir in these words? Circle the object in which you can't hear Irving Ir saying his last name.

Think of an '**ir**' word and draw it.

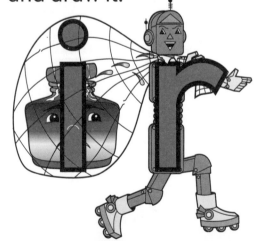

Circle the '**ir**' word that rhymes in each row.

bird

flower

3rd
third

purse

skirt

shirt

hammer

shorts

30
thirty

spray

bath

dirty

girl

garden

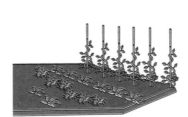
twirl

fern

Can you hear Urgent Ur in these words? Circle the object in which you can't hear Urgent Ur saying his last name.

Think of an '**ur**' word and draw it.

Look at the pictures. Choose the correct '**ur**' word to complete the sentences and write in on the line.

Max will see the nurse on

Tuesday

Thursday

Friday

_____ .

The teddy has got

purple fur

yellow fur

blue fur

_____ .

Tess has a drink and a

peach

burger

cake

_____ .

Write '**ur**' or '**ir**' on the lines to complete these words.

ur   ir

b___ d

ur   ir

n___ se

ur   ir

f___

ur   ir

sh___ t

Find the objects that include Red Robot and Walter Walrus. Tick a box as you find each one.

write

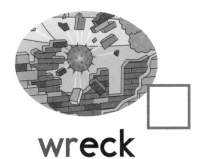

wreck

wrapper

Can you hear Red Robot capturing Walter Walrus in these words? Circle the object in which you can't hear Red Robot capturing Walter Walrus.

Think of a '**wr**' word and draw it.

Draw a line around the '**wr**' words in the grid below. They go across and down.

write

wreck

wring

wrapper

wriggle

Can you find one more '**wr**' word in the grid? Copy it on to the lines.

___ ___ ___ ___ ___

Sticker

Use your stickers to label the picture below.
These are all words you know.

Write down one more word
you can see in the picture
that has an **er**, **ir** or **ur** sound.

Read each sentence. Look at the four other words and see if you can substitute one or two words to make a new sentence.

1

His car did not start.	boat	horse	eat	jump

Example: His horse did not jump.

....

....

2

She eats fish with a fork.	jam	spoon	cat	he

....

....

3

He likes sport on Sunday.	Friday	arm	she	singing

....

....

4

The scarf is for Arthur.	dark	dog	card	Mark

....

....

Pair work Write your new sentences on the lines. Then read them to your partner. Your partner can decide if the new sentence makes sense!

Listen Listen to the words and put a tick next to the one you hear. The first one has been done for you.

Track
145

1.  ✔ ☐ ☐

2.  ☐ ☐  ☐

3.  ☐ ☐ 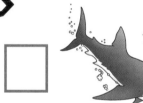 ☐

4.  ☐  ☐  ☐

5.  ☐ ☐ 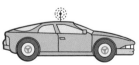 ☐

Listen again

This exercise requires careful listening skills. Listen more than once if you need to.

Listen to the words. Put a tick next to the correct spelling pattern. The first one has been done for you.

Track 146

How do you spell it?

1.  **ar** ✓    **or** ☐    **wr** ☐

2.  **er** ☐    **ir** ☐    **ur** ☐

3.  **er** ☐    **ir** ☐   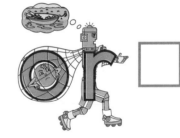 **or** ☐

4.  **er** ☐    **ir** ☐    **ur** ☐

5.  **ar** ☐    **er** ☐    **wr** ☐

Listen again

This exercise requires careful listening skills. Listen more than once if you need to.

Find the objects that include Oscar's Bothersome Little Brother. Tick a box as you find each one.

 monkey

 son

 money

Draw lines from Oscar's Bothersome Little Brother to the things that include him saying **o**. Circle the one that doesn't.

Think of an '**o**' word and draw it.

Write **o** on the lines to complete these words.

s _ n

h _ ney

m _ ney

m _ nkey

d _ ve

Can you think of any more Bothers**o**me Little Br**o**ther words?

Draw lines from the Foot Twin to the things that include his sound. Circle the one where the Boot Twin is talking.

Think of a **Foo**t Twin word and draw it.

Circle the **oo** word that rhymes in each row.

wood

zoo

van

hood

cook

cake

corn

look

foot

fruit

soot

goose

book

hook

bug

bricks

Draw lines to join each picture to the correct word.

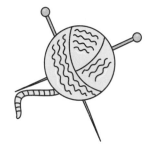

foot

wood

book

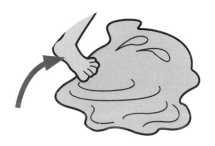

hood

wool

cookie

Find the objects that include Upside Down Umbrella. Tick a box as you find each one.

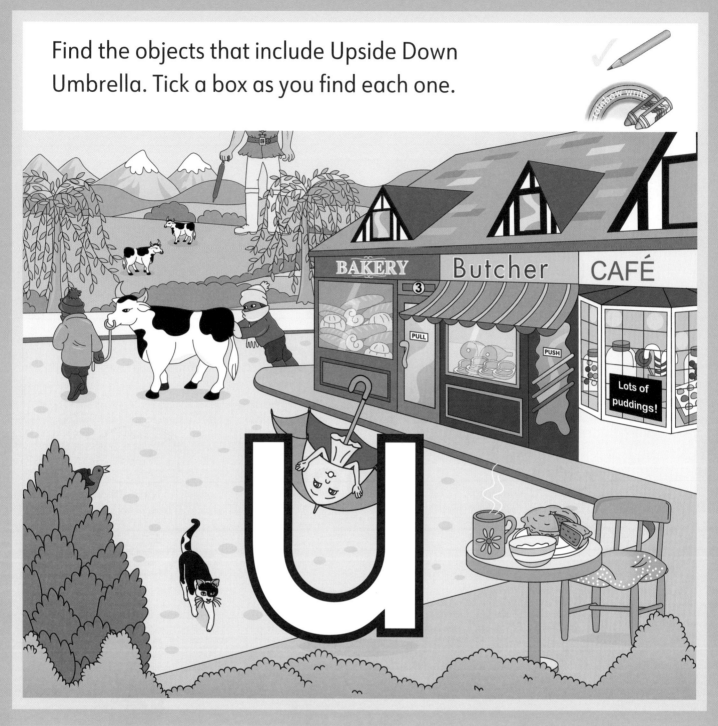

p**u**sh

p**u**ll

s**u**gar

Draw lines from Upside Down Umbrella to the things that include her sound. Circle the one that doesn't.

Think of an '**u**' word and draw it.

Circle the **u** word that rhymes in each row.

push

toys

bush

wool

pull

monkey

book

bull

money

wood

honey

oil

Find the words that include Roy and the Yo-yo Man.
Tick a box as you find each one.

toys

boy

soy

Draw lines from Roy and the Yo-yo Man to the things that include their **oy** sound. Circle the one that doesn't.

Think of an '**oy**' word and draw it.

Fill in the missing words to complete the sentences.
The words you need are in the yellow space below.

This _____

is _____ .

The _____ are

on a _____ .

annoyed boy toys voyage

Draw lines from Roy and Mr I to the things that include their **oi** sound. Circle the one that doesn't.

Think of an **oi** word and draw it.

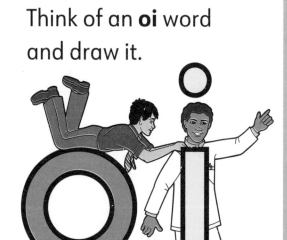

Draw a line around the **oi** words in the grid below. They go across and down.

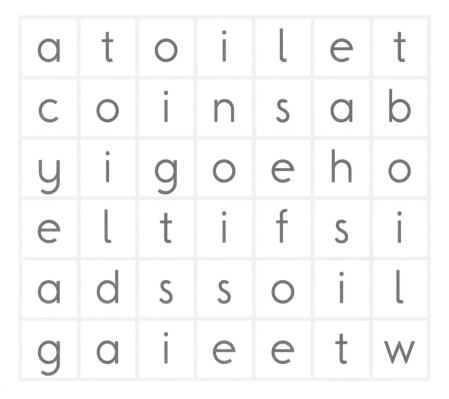

a	t	o	i	l	e	t	
c	o	i	n	s	a	b	
y	i	g	o	e	h	o	
e	l	t	i	f	s	i	
a	d	s	s	o	i	l	
g	a	i	e	e	t	w	

soil

toilet

noise

coins

oil

Can you find one more
oi word in the grid?
Copy it on to the lines.

___ ___ ___ ___

Write **oi** on the lines to complete these words.

s___l   b___l

n___se

c___ns   ___l

Can you think of any more **oi** words?

Write down one more word you can see in the picture that has an

oo, **oy** or **oi** sound.

Clue: It's in the Queen's bag.

Find the words

How many more words can you think of that contain '**oo**', '**oy**' and '**oi**'?

 Listen to the words. Put a tick next to the correct spelling pattern. The first one has been done for you.

 Track 170

How do you spell it?

1.  ☐   ☐    ✔

2.  ☐   ☐    ☐

3.  ☐    ☐    ☐

4.  ☐    ☐    ☐

5.  ☐    ☐    ☐

Listen

Listen to the words and put a tick next to the one you hear.

Track 171

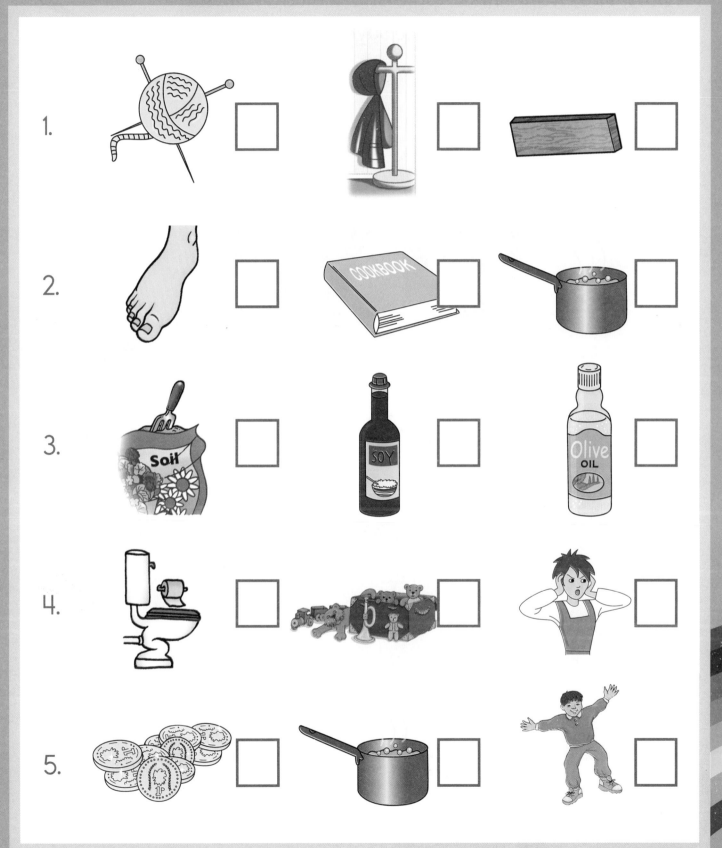

Listen again

This exercise requires careful listening skills. Review the words from the previous pages. Then listen again, more than once if you need to.

57

Draw lines from Annie Apple and Walter Walrus to the things that include Annie saying **aw**! Circle the one that doesn't.

Think of an **aw** word and draw it.

Look at the pictures below and draw a circle around each difference in picture 2.

1

2

Answers: 1. The jigsaw has moved; 2. A strawberry plant is missing; 3. The saw handle is red; 4. The straw is missing; 5. The trawler boat is missing. 6. The coleslaw is missing.

Fill in the missing words to complete the sentences.
The words you need are in the yellow space below.

The vet _____ the cat
had hurt its _____.

Dippy can _____
a _____.

draw   paw   saw   strawberry

Draw lines from Annie Apple and Walter in Uppy's letter to the things that include Annie saying '**au**'! Circle the one that doesn't.

CAUTION
ROCKET
LAUNCH

Think of an '**au**' word and draw it.

61

Draw a line around the **au** words in the grid below. They go across and down.

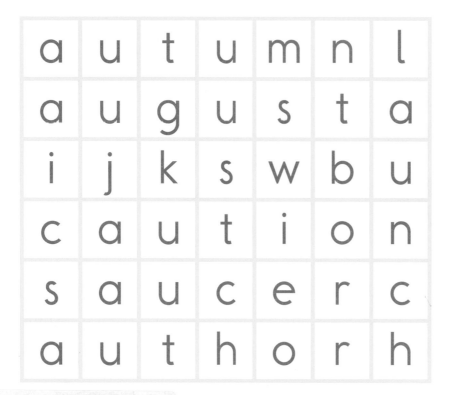

launch

author

caution

autumn

August

Can you find one more **au** word in the grid? Copy it on to the lines.

_____ _____ _____ _____ _____ _____

Write **aw** or **au** on the lines to complete these words.

aw   au

str____

aw   au

l___nch

aw   au

s___cer

aw   au

y___n

Use your stickers to label the picture below. Look back in your book if you need help remembering the words.

Write down what season you think it is in this scene.

_____ _____ _____ _____ _____ _____

Read each sentence. Look at the four other words and see if you can substitute one or two words to make a new sentence.

1

| I saw an ant jump. | boy | a | astronaut | yawn |

Example: I saw a boy jump.

....

....

2

| This cat has four paws. | man | dog | lots of | claws |

....

3

| Let's find a clean saucer. | straw | new | get | jigsaw |

....

4

| It can be windy in autumn. | cold | August | hot | winter |

....

Pair work

Write your new sentences on the lines. Then read them to your partner. Your partner can decide if the new sentence makes sense!

Listen

Listen to the words and put a tick next to the one you hear.

Track
182

1.

2.

3.

4.

5.

Listen again

This exercise requires careful listening skills. Review the words from the previous pages. Then listen again, more than once if you need to.

How do you spell it?

1.  ✔   ☐

2. ☐   ☐

3. ☐   ☐

4. ☐   ☐

5. ☐   ☐

Listen again This exercise requires careful listening skills. As you listen, think how the word looks. Look back to earlier pages if you need to.

Draw lines from Oscar Orange and Walter Walrus to the things that include them howling **ow**! Circle the one that doesn't.

Think of an '**ow**' word and draw it.

Circle the **ow** word that rhymes in each row.

vowels

van

towels

torch

clown

town

clock

toys

shower

ship

fan

flower

brown

blue

crown

house

Look at the pictures below. Tick a box for each difference in picture 2.

1

2

Draw lines from Oscar Orange and Walter in Uppy's letter to the things that include them shouting **ou**! Circle the one that doesn't.

Think of an '**ou**' word and draw it.

Draw a line around the **ou** words in the grid below. They go across and down.

v	d	m	a	o	f	m
c	l	o	u	d	s	o
e	o	u	i	f	c	u
w	u	t	p	s	k	s
y	d	h	o	u	s	e
s	h	o	u	t	s	g

mouth

house

loud

mouse

clouds

Can you find one more **ou** word in the grid? Copy it on to the lines.

_____ _____ _____ _____ _____

Write **ou** on the lines to complete these words.

m___th

h___se

m___ntain

m___se   cl___ds

Can you think of any more **ou** words?

Use your stickers to label the picture below. Look back in your book if you need help remembering the words.

Write down where this scene is.

_____ _____ _____ _____

Read each sentence. Look at the four other words and see if you can substitute one or two words to make a new sentence.

1

The brown cow ate a flower.	cat	black	sat on	mouse

Example: The brown cat ate a mouse.

....

....

2

Take a towel to the shower.	town	dog	house	park

....

3

There's a mouse in the house.	towel	ground	cow	on

....

4

Count the vowels in the word.	letters	sentence	find	mouse

....

Listen  Listen to the words. Put a tick next to the correct spelling pattern. The first one has been done for you.

Track
192

How do you spell it?

1.  ✔    ☐

2.  ☐    ☐

3.  ☐    ☐

4.  ☐    ☐

5.  ☐    ☐

Listen again This exercise requires careful listening skills. As you listen, think how the word looks. Look back to earlier pages if you need to.

Read and trace the words below.
Then draw the picture.

 house

 vowels

 cow

 clouds

 mouse

 flower

You can read lots of words now! Try reading all of the phrases below. Do this exercise as a test with your teacher.

For teacher's marks only.

I like chips with my fish. ☐

Let's play games on the train. ☐

Green peas in a scene. ☐

Flies like the light at night. ☐

That goat ate the yellow roses. ☐

At school I play new flute tunes. ☐

Garden fork sale starts soon. ☐

It is my sister's third birthday. ☐

Fluency Read the sentences slowly at first. Then read them again faster. Try to add expression, too!

Test me!

 **Write**

Listen to the word twice, then try to write it down.
The first one has been done for you.

Track
193

For teacher's marks only.

1. cake ☐

2. ☐

3. ☐

4. ☐

5. ☐

6. ☐

7. ☐

8. ☐

Listen & write

Listen again if you need to. You can spell a lot of words now.
Well done!

Test me!

79

Certificate!

This is to certify that

....

has finished

LETTERLAND® Fix-it Phonics Level 2

....

Your Letterland Teacher

....

Date

www.letterland.com